ICNC **SPECIAL REPORT** SERIES

Sudan's 2019 Revolution

The Power of Civil Resistance

Stephen Zunes

Table of Contents

I. Introduction 1

II. **Chronology** 3
    A. Prior to the 2018-19 Revolution 3
    B. The Initial Uprising 4
    C. Bashir's Ouster and Aftermath 7
    D. The Sit-in at Military Headquarters 8
    E. Resistance Intensifies 10
    F. Negotiations and Settlement 11

III. **Nonviolent Discipline** 12
    A. Enforcing Nonviolent Discipline 13
    B. Nonviolent Training 14

IV. **Other Factors Contributing to Success** 16
    A. Breadth and Depth of Civil Resistance 16
    B. Local Resistance Committees 17
    C. The Role of Women 19
    D. Effective Messaging 20
    E. Social Media 22
    F. Security Force Defections 23
    G. Tactical Innovations 24
    H. Structural Factors 26

V. **Post-Revolutionary Transition and the Role of a Mobilized People** 28

VI. **Lessons Learned** 32

VII. **Conclusion** 35

".... from the beginning we understood that the only weapon we have is nonviolence. This is the weapon that we have and they don't. They wanted to put us in a bottle by using violence. We knew that if we reacted with violence we would lose. We understood well that nonviolence is the only 'weapon' that they do not have."[1] —HASHIM MATTAR

INTRODUCTION

IT IS PERHAPS FITTING that one of the greatest stories of the power of nonviolent resistance came out of a country notorious for decades of horrific state-sanctioned violence. Or that women would take such impressive leadership in a country known for its particularly misogynistic laws. Or that there could be such unity in a country long divided by religion, ethnicity, and region. Or that there could emerge an impressive level of participation by a population systematically disempowered through decades of dictatorship. The scenes of millions of Sudanese out on the streets during waves of protests over an eight-month period in 2018-2019 demonstrate a triumph not just of the human spirit, but of some of the most brilliant strategic thinking by any social movement in history.

Sudan did not fit into what some Western analysts would see as the conditions necessary for a successful pro-democracy civil resistance movement. The regime, consisting of a coalition of ultra-conservative Islamists and right-wing military officers under the leadership of General Omar al-Bashir, had been in power for nearly thirty years. It was widely believed to be too oppressive, too entrenched, and too successful in its divide-and-rule tactics of the large and ethnically heterogeneous nation to be vulnerable to a civil insurrection. Their reactionary limitations on women's rights had seemingly disempowered half the population. The country's once-vibrant civil society had been decimated under the three decades of military rule, and the Sudanese people were seen as too impoverished, uneducated, and isolated to mobilize successfully. Millions of the country's most educated and ambitious potential leaders had emigrated. Wealthy Gulf monarchies were helping to prop up the Sudanese military regime. And most of the West had largely written off Sudan as a hopeless case, with a number of countries maintaining strict sanctions on Sudan that hurt the people more than the government.

It was Sudanese civil society organizations, particularly labor unions, that played a critical role in the successful pro-democracy uprisings against military dictatorships in 1964 and 1985. However, with unions and other independent organizations—from human rights groups to

---

[1] Interview, Hashim Mattar, Khartoum North, January 8, 2020.

the Rotary Club—suppressed by the regime, organizing was extremely challenging. The independent business sector was limited as well, with the government making it very difficult to run a successful company unless it was clearly pro-regime. Opposition political parties were severely restricted in their activities and the older, more established parties had little credibility or support among younger Sudanese.

Despite this, starting in December 2018, Sudanese citizens took to the streets to protest in the face of severe repression. By April 2019, al-Bashir had been overthrown by fellow military officers, who had come under mounting pressure from millions of irrepressible protesters. Protests for change continued, despite hundreds of civilian deaths, and by August the military stepped down to make way for a civilian-led transitional government.

This report reviews the chronology of the resistance struggle in Sudan, the critical role of nonviolent discipline, other factors contributing to the movement's success, and the current political situation. It seeks to explain how the movement was able to succeed despite enormous odds against it and what lessons could be learned by those facing similarly difficult circumstances.

Given the serious challenges facing the new civilian-led government, there is a real possibility that—as was the case following successful pro-democracy struggles decades earlier—the military could again seize power. However, as will be elaborated below, there are also reasons for hope that this time democratic forces will indeed remain successful in the long run.

Chronology

Prior to the 2018-19 Revolution

Sudan is unusual in its history of civil insurrections. Nonviolent movements played a key role in the country's anti-colonial struggle which led to Sudan's independence from Great Britain in 1956. Long before the Arab Spring, the Eastern European revolutions, and other popular democratic uprisings which caught the world's attention, the Sudanese had toppled dictatorships in both 1964 and 1985 through massive civil resistance campaigns. The dictatorship which seized power in 1985, however, was particularly brutal and effective in its consolidation of power, systematically dismantling civil society institutions which had played such an important role in the previous uprisings. The discovery of oil in 1998 strengthened the state apparatus further. Despite this, there had been unarmed uprisings in 2011, 2012, 2013, and 2016, though all of them proved unsuccessful.

The wave of protests that began in 2011 was the culmination of years of effort to carve out some degree of political space for opponents of the regime, starting with the universities. One such struggle began ten years earlier, led by students demanding free elections for leadership positions in the student union, who launched a series of protests, boycotts, and sit-ins. In 2003, the government finally allowed for free elections at the universities and oppositionists won some of them, including at the University of Khartoum, the country's largest and most prestigious academic institution. In autocratic societies, achieving what might seem to be small victories that bring about a limited democratic opening, such as free student elections, can in fact play an important role in paving the way for future major victories. One of the student activists from that period who was involved in organizing observed: "The lesson learned at that time is to keep working, keep pushing and organizing people in the grassroots using different tools and tactics. Try to widen the space for civic engagement and eventually a movement will emerge."[2]

Though the overall political system remained highly repressive and authoritarian, the interim constitution passed in 2005 in an effort to curb the ongoing rebellion in the south had opened up some civic and political space. However, the organized political parties were weak and divided and thus unable to attract support from younger Sudanese.

Still, the gradual opening of political space at universities and elsewhere was taken full advantage of by civil society members to set the stage for the wave of protests in the 2010s, the largest of which took place in 2013. That uprising, however, was brutally suppressed within weeks. Following this failed mobilization, the Sudan Call was organized in December 2014, signed by such leading opposition groups as the National Consensus Forces (NCF),

---

2   Interview, Khaled Omar Yousif, Khartoum, January 12, 2020.

the Sudan Revolutionary Front (SRF), the National Umma Party (NUP), and the newly-formed Civil Society Initiative (CSI) led by a renowned human rights lawyer and activist. The Call demanded an end to one-party rule and the establishment of a transitional government that would lead to a constitutional process and prepare for national elections. Determined not to repeat the mistakes of 2013, they recognized the importance of establishing clear leadership and greater unity in order for the movement to be successful. Meanwhile, the Sudanese Professionals Association held a series of seminars and research projects to raise consciousness and build constituencies.

By the time the uprising emerged in December 2018, organized opposition was growing, but much of the opposition was still divided between those who were willing to participate in upcoming elections and those who called for more active resistance outside of institutional channels. Neither seemed to have a clear vision of a path forward. However, professional unions came to the fore to take on leadership roles in organizing the resistance and putting forth clear demands. On January 1, 2019, less than two weeks after the initial 2018 protests, the first coordinating committee came together consisting of Sudan Call, the Sudanese Professionals Association (SPA), Sudan Revolutionary Front, No to Oppression against Women Initiative, Women of Sudanese Civic and Political Groups (MANSAM), National Consensus Forces, and the Unionist Gathering. The committee called itself the Forces of Freedom and Change (FFC) and served as the main coordinating body for the revolutionary struggle. The original January 1, 2019 declaration was joined by 150 other groups, some of which were already coalitions, each of them nominating representatives to the coordinating committee. In signing on, this impressive number of institutional and grassroots organizations demonstrated that a huge swathe of civil society was not just concerned about the economic crisis, which prompted the initial protests, but was ready to demand fundamental political change.[3] The SPA, an association of seventeen primarily middle-class unions, played a particularly important role within the FFC during the course of the struggle.

The Initial Uprising

The protests which culminated in the regime's overthrow did not begin in the capital, but began in Ad-Damazin, a small city in the southeast, on December 12, 2018, in response to the tripling of the price of bread. Angry protests erupted a week later in Atbara, a smaller city in the northeast which, as a center of the country's important rail industry once known for its leftist trade union activities, proved to be a spark, leading to protests quickly spreading to the cities of Dongola and Port Sudan. In what was to be an exception in the overwhelmingly nonviolent revolution, protesters set fire to the ruling party headquarters in Atbara and

---

3   Sudanese Professionals Association, "Declaration of Freedom and Change," Khartoum, January 1, 2019, https://www.sudaneseprofessionals.org/en/declaration-of-freedom-and-change/.

Dongola. In response, police killed a number of demonstrators. Within two days, as protests grew, the government closed schools, imposed curfews, and shut off access to social media and instant messaging platforms such as Facebook, Twitter, Instagram, and WhatsApp.

However, the protests spread nationwide in subsequent weeks. In February, Bashir declared a state of emergency, replaced regional governors with military generals, imposed stricter censorship of the press, and violently suppressed demonstrators. Despite all this, the FFC continued organizing protests and other resistance actions, putting out weekly action timetables every Thursday night. With strict limitations on people's movement enforced by military checkpoints on roads, oppositionists kept the resistance alive by mobilizing at the neighborhood level, organizing rallies in soccer fields or other public spaces, sometimes at odd hours. FFC activist Khaled Omar Yousif noted, "We started the protests inside the neighborhoods to show that we were resisting this regime everywhere. They were often very small and took place at night. The idea was to bring more people into the movement by giving everyone a tool to resist."[4] A colleague of his noted that by making resistance of the regime local and relatively low-risk, "even old women and many children nearby could gather and at least join in the singing."[5] The decentralized nature of the resistance, including at the village level, had the advantage of spreading the protests wide enough throughout the country that the repressive apparatus of the regime couldn't respond. It provided what Yousif described as "a day for the villages, [rather than] the cities, which gave people in the rural areas the opportunity to participate in the movement."[6] By March, demonstrations had broken out in at least fifteen of Sudan's eighteen states. Reem Abbas wrote, "The protests were a tremendous geography lesson for all of us, as we would discover a new village or town we'd never heard of after seeing news of protests erupting there or watching a live-video feed."[7]

> "We started the protests inside the neighborhoods to show that we were resisting this regime everywhere. The idea was to bring more people into the movement by giving everyone a tool to resist."

At the same time, some of the leading activists began to question the impact of small protests in remote areas, even if the protests engaged a proportionally impressive percentage of the surrounding population. Yousif observed, "These protests started to lose momentum by the end of February, so we started to think that we cannot go for an indefinite time doing the same thing. People are going to be tired and lose hope that nothing is going to

---

4   Interview, Khaled Omar Yousif, Khartoum, January 12, 2020.

5   Interview, Ahmed Salman, Khartoum, January 12, 2020.

6   Interview, Khaled Omar Yousif, Khartoum, January 12, 2020.

7   Reem Abbas, "Sudan's Unfinished Revolution: The Dictator Is Gone, but the Fight Continues," *The Nation*, April 26, 2019.

happen." To avoid the mistake made by some movements of repeating the same tactics for too long, the leadership recognized it was time to escalate the nonviolent resistance, especially when there was evidence, according to Yousif, "that the divisions inside the regime started to be very clear." Consequently, "we decided to prepare for a big day to march towards the headquarters of the army."[8]

Indeed, at this point, the remarkably large number of Sudanese involved in the protests, the organizational strength of the opposition, the tenacity of the demonstrators, and the breadth of the movement in terms of geography, ethnicity, and gender had convinced some elements of the ruling elite that this movement would not be easily crushed like the previous uprisings. Divisions within the ruling circles were becoming evident. The right-wing Islamist National Congress Party (NCP), which was the primary civilian base of Bashir's rule, called for him to step down, and there were growing reports of moves within the military and intelligence services to push Bashir aside. Bashir decided to leave the NCP, which he had once led, with the apparent hope of gaining support from the military. As a result, three and a half months into the uprising, the pro-democracy activists decided it was time to confront the military directly in setting up a dilemma action. According to Yousif:

When we decided to go to the army headquarters on the 6th of April, the idea behind it was to test the army itself, to force them to choose between two tough decisions: They either support Bashir by shooting thousands of peaceful protestors or we reach through to them, pushing open the cracks inside the army itself to force Bashir to step down.[9]

As many as 800,000 protesters descended on the military complex, the most dangerous place in the nation's capital, on April 6, the 34th anniversary of former president Yaafar al-Numeiry's ouster. The remarkable number of citizens participating in the protest astonished even the protest organizers. The emotional impact for those who had suffered under three decades of dictatorship was palpable. One participant wrote, "An old colleague I hadn't seen in years saw me and said, 'I was waiting to see someone I know because I want to cry.' We held each other and cried. Everyone around us was crying and chanting."[10]

Divisions within the armed forces became apparent that day when the regime ordered the army to stop a large column of protesters coming from the north, but troops refused the orders to fire. Yousif continues:

---

8 Interview, Khaled Omar Yousif, Khartoum, January 12, 2020.

9 Ibid.

10 Reem Abbas, "Sudan's Unfinished Revolution: The Dictator Is Gone, but the Fight Continues," *The Nation*, April 26, 2019.

We managed to succeed and reach the army headquarters, but there was no plan or serious idea of having a sit-in there. But the numbers of people who reached the headquarters of the army on April 6 were astonishing. We made the decision [almost instantly] that we should right now announce a sit-in in front of the army's headquarters asking them to take the side of the people and to force Bashir to step down.[11]

At that point, the SPA released a statement saying, "At this historic moment, we urge you to stay the course on the streets surrounding the Headquarters of the Armed Forces, and in every site across the country, until the tyranny is dismantled once and for all."[12] In a desperate effort to cut off communication between oppositionists, power was shut off throughout the country, but the numbers of protesters in the boulevard and open spaces near the headquarters continued to swell dramatically, estimated to reach in the millions.[13]

Bashir's Ouster and Aftermath

On April 11, the sixth day of the sit-in, the military ousted Bashir, placing him under house arrest and announcing the formation of a Transitional Military Council (TMC). They also announced the release of all political prisoners, including those arrested in the protests.

Unlike in Egypt, where the opposition naively trusted that the military would oversee a successful transition to democracy, the Sudanese demanded the TMC step down and allow for civilian leadership. Particularly controversial was the naming of Lt. Gen. Awad Ibn Auf, a war criminal and close confidant of Bashir, as TMC head. On the streets, the popular anti-Bashir chant "Fall, that's all!" was replaced by "Fall, again!" amongst protesters. The level of defiance to TMC rule quickly became apparent when the TMC announced a curfew between the hours of 10:00pm and 4:00am but many protesters remained camped out.

It took only a day of resistance for Ibn Auf to resign. His replacement, Army Inspector General Abdel Fattah al-Burhan, was one of the few generals who had been in communication with the protesters during the sit-in. The following day, April 13, the curfew order was lifted, the despised intelligence chief Salah Gosh was dismissed, and formal talks between the protesters and the military began. Abbas noted: "After 30 years of being told that the Ingaz (that's what Bashir's government had called itself) was everlasting, and that even God

---

11 Interview, Khaled Omar Yousif, Khartoum, January, 12, 2020.

12 Cited in Reem Abbas, "Sudan's Unfinished Revolution: The Dictator Is Gone, but the Fight Continues," *The Nation*, April 26, 2019.

13 Interview, Hashim Mattar, Khartoum North, January 8, 2020.

couldn't change it, people regained their confidence. They had toppled two rulers within two days. So there was a new chant: 'It fell twice, it will fall again.'"[14]

Over the next several days, a number of the more notorious members of Bashir's regime were dismissed or detained, but protesters were still adamant in their call for a transition to civilian rule. In response to calls from the FFC, millions took to the streets nationwide shouting "Power to civilians! Power to civilians!" in the largest demonstration to date. On April 23, in what became an iconic image of the revolution, hundreds of protesters filling the railway cars and, riding on the roof of a train coming in from Atabar—seen as the birthplace of the revolution—arrived in Khartoum to join the sit-in. Delegations from Darfur, eastern Sudan, Kordofan, the Blue Nile, and elsewhere in the country joined the sit-in.

Concurrently, a series of strikes spread nationwide, including in Port Sudan, the country's only major outlet to the sea, where striking workers blockaded the port. Smaller sit-ins began in other cities across the country.

The Sit-in at Military Headquarters

Rather than a public square, major boulevard, or other government offices, the choice of the large area in front of the military headquarters—consisting of three major buildings for each branch of the armed services—became the central rallying point for the resistance. Access to the area is normally restricted and taking photos is not permitted, so there was strong symbolism in the creation of what amounted to a free speech zone. It was close to the University of Khartoum and the Burri neighborhood, known for activism during the struggle. The choice of that location, under the watch of the armed services, also made clear that should any harm come to the peaceful protesters, it would be the military that was ultimately responsible.

A series of functional committees were set up to manage life in encampment. The Protection Committee ran overall security, set up barricades, and supervised the checkpoints. The Provisions Committees organized food and drink for protesters. The Medical Committees provided treatment for the injured. The Awareness Raising Committee educated participants about their rights as Sudanese to peace, freedom, justice and democracy as well as the importance of nonviolent discipline. Another committee was responsible for collecting garbage and keeping the area sanitary. The Organization Committee oversaw the other committees and distribution of membership. Meanwhile, discussion circles were set up to tackle such issues as combatting discrimination based on race, ethnicity, religion, and gender. Mural projects and other artistic endeavors became an important focus.

---

14   Reem Abbas, "Sudan's Unfinished Revolution: The Dictator Is Gone, but the Fight Continues," *The Nation*, April 26, 2019.

The level of organization and community support in the encampments was remarkable. Classrooms were organized, makeshift health clinics provided medicine and treatments, toilets and other sanitation facilities were set up, and accommodations were made for homeless children and adults. Five large kitchens, using food donated by farmers and herders, cooked and served meals to the protesters. Water stations were set up to keep people hydrated in the hot sun. Street peddlers circulated in the crowd. Entertainers performed and opposition politicians spoke from a large stage that was erected. Cultural activities such as art projects, drumming circles, poetry and music were a constant feature. International supporters gave interviews and provided statements of solidarity which were broadcast on a large screen, which also would occasionally show soccer matches and other entertainment.[15] Women were free to go without a headscarf and young people of different genders were allowed to hang out together—activities which were illegal outside the encampment. It provided a space where, for the first time in decades, ordinary Sudanese could talk about politics without fear.

According to a BBC interview with activist Dalia El Roubi at the time,

The types of people participating are so diverse—a mix of ages, religions, classes, ethnicities and gender. Being in there, none of us feel alone in this cause. People are peaceful, helpful and protective of one another. This sit-in shows a lot of who we are as a nation—our resilience, courage, solidarity, community and commitment to change our country.[16]

This harmonious encampment symbolized the idea of what a future Sudan and Sudanese society could look like, if built on the principles of equality, transparency, open deliberation and participation, non-discrimination, and nonviolent action.

The sit-in continued into June, albeit in smaller numbers, amid on-and-off negotiations with the TMC. There were several attempts to dislodge the protesters, resulting in a number of civilian deaths. The continued strength of the pro-democracy uprising was demonstrated in a two-day general strike on May 28-29. The strike was organized by the FFC and paralyzed much of the country, closing markets, shops, restaurants, banks, factories, public transit, and air travel. The ongoing sit-in of many thousands in front of the military headquarters, supported by neighborhood committees throughout the greater Khartoum area, kept the demand for civilian rule in the public's focus.

---

15 Amira Osman, "Sudan: the symbolic significance of the space protesters made their own," *The Conversation*, April 26, 2019, **https://theconversation.com/sudan-the-symbolic-significance-of-the-space-protesters-made-their-own-115864**.

16 Interview, Dalia el-Roubi, "Sudan protests: Inside the sit-in at army HQ," *BBC News*, April 9, 2019, **https://www.bbc.com/news/world-africa-47869171.**

With the loyalty of the regular army and police in question, the TMC had to rely on the notoriously repressive National Intelligence and Security Service (NISS) to destroy the encampment in the apparent hope that it would cripple the movement's morale and focus. Before dawn on June 3, the Rapid Support Forces (the paramilitary unit of the NISS, formerly known as the Janjaweed) launched a full-scale attack, dispersing the sit-in and killing over one hundred protesters. Many hundreds more were wounded or arrested, and seventy men and women were raped. Several soldiers who refused to engage in the massacre were themselves shot and killed.[17] Sit-ins in Port Sudan, Sinja, and El-Gadarif were also violently dispersed.

Resistance Intensifies

If the TMC had hoped such severe repression would terrorize the population into submission, it failed to consider the willingness of the opposition to continue to resist. In the massacre's immediate aftermath, the Sudanese Professionals Association (SPA), a leading component of the FFC, released a statement calling for:

- Complete civil disobedience; closing of all main streets, bridges and openings; and bringing public life to a general halt.

- Open political strike at all places of work and facilities, in the public and private sectors.

- Continuous work, coordination, and strong organization through neighborhood committees and strike committees.

- Holding to the principle of nonviolent resistance in all our direct actions, towards change.[18]

A three-day general strike starting on June 9, 2019, was heeded by a sizable majority of Sudanese nationwide, as evidenced by large-scale absences of pupils and teachers from elementary and high schools; the closure of municipal and intercity bus transport; the near-complete cessation of rail transport and air travel; non-publication of newspapers; and the closure of banks, shops, gas stations, legal services, and non-emergency medical services. The government once again shut down the internet and began arresting activists. Despite the horror of the massacre and the escalation of the repression, SPA's statement declared, "We call upon our Sudanese people to be steadfast in their commitment to nonviolent resistance, as it is our strong fort and superior weapon, and to refuse the attempts of the coup council to draw the whole country towards violence and counter violence."[19]

---

17 Nermin Ismail, "Militiamen in Sudan raped men and women, says eyewitness," *DW*, June 9, 2019, **https://www.dw.com/en/militiamen-in-sudan-raped-men-and-women-says-eyewitness/a-49120693.**

18 Sudan Professionals Association, "Complete civil disobedience, and open political strike, to avoid chaos," June 4, 2019, **https://www.sudaneseprofessionals.org/en/complete-civil-disobedience-and-open-political-strike-to-avoid-chaos/.**

19 Interview, Hashim Mattar, Khartoum North, January 8, 2020.

The willingness of the opposition to not only continue but escalate their nonviolent resistance following the massacre seemed to underscore to the military that they would have to engage in even more massive violence in an attempt to suppress the rebellion, further discrediting themselves domestically and internationally, and putting themselves in an even more untenable situation. Realizing that more violence was unlikely to achieve its desired results, the TMC agreed to release arrested protesters and resume talks. Periodic protests continued, some met by severe repression.

The regime's ongoing blocking of the internet forced activists to redouble their offline organizing efforts to demand a transition to civilian rule. On June 30, millions of Sudanese took to the streets in cities across the country to demand justice and accountability for those killed and the transfer of power to a civilian-led government in what may be one of the largest mass protests in world history relative to a country's population.

Negotiations and Settlement

Talks between the FFC and the TMC resumed, facilitated by the African Union and the Ethiopian government. The pro-democracy movement recognized they simply did not have the strength to completely oust the military from positions of power or to defeat the combined forces of the NISS, the right-wing Islamists, and the army. At the same time, the success of the general strike and the June 30 demonstration helped the military recognize that they could not defeat the opposition, which clearly would not settle for anything less than civilian leadership. Additionally, international pressure was building to isolate the government diplomatically, as evidenced by the African Union's decision to suspend Sudan's membership.[20]

While willing to allow civilians to take roles in government, there was strong resistance within the military to allow civilians to dominate it. Another point of contention was accountability for the killings and other human rights abuses committed during the previous months.

With the pillars of support for the regime weakening and collapsing, including leading pro-regime oligarchs shifting to the opposition, a divided military leadership finally agreed to give up their monopoly on power. A tentative agreement between the TMC and the FFC on the establishment of a civilian-led government was reached a week later on July 5. The agreement was finalized and formally signed on July 17. The new government consisting of both civilian and military representatives in the governing bodies, but led by a civilian prime minister and cabinet officials, came to power by the end of August 2019.

---

20   Jason Burke, "African Union suspends Sudan over violence against protesters," *The Guardian*, June 6, 2019, **https://www.theguardian.com/world/2019/jun/06/sudan-african-union-suspension-military-rulers.**

Nonviolent Discipline

Perhaps the single most important factor leading to the victory of pro-democracy forces was nonviolent discipline. Remaining nonviolent despite enormous provocations made it difficult for the regime to depict the movement in a negative light, helped the movement gain sympathy it would have otherwise lost through violent tactics, and made it possible for people to feel more comfortable joining the protests, thereby increasing the movement's numbers. When protesters were met by police or other security forces, they would chant, *"Silmiya! Silmiya!"* ("Peaceful! Peaceful!") to reassure them of their intent in an effort to defuse the situation. The opposition stressed the importance of maintaining nonviolent discipline not out of any moral commitment to nonviolence per se, but because of an understanding that tactically and strategically it was the most likely path to victory. Had the movement used violence, the regime would always have the advantage. By choosing what amounted to a different weapons system—protests, sit-ins, strikes, and more—their opponents were unable to depict the protesters as terrorists who would plunge the country into violence and chaos.

Remaining nonviolent made it difficult for the regime to depict the movement in a negative light and helped it gain sympathy otherwise lost through violent tactics.

The Sudanese opposition had engaged in violent struggle previously. Beginning in 1993, operating out of bases in Eritrea, an armed guerrilla movement was launched. Despite the support of major opposition parties, it never got far, failing to provoke a more widespread popular uprising. This lack of active support from the population combined with successful counter-insurgency operations by the regime led to the violent rebellion's defeat in 2005. Ongoing armed resistance by separatists in Darfur in the west, the Nuba Mountains in South Kordofan, and the Blue Nile region in the southeast also failed to weaken the regime or spread beyond those regions and were met by brutal counter-insurgency operations.

The civil insurrection of 2013 included widespread rioting and was crushed within days after scores of civilian deaths. The government's use of agents provocateurs in that rebellion, who destroyed cars, burned gas stations, and engaged in other acts of vandalism, was an indication that the regime preferred an opposition that would engage in violence. As a result of the broad understanding that the rioting of 2013 was counter-productive, there was a conscious decision to choose a different path.[21] Seeing how both armed struggle and rioting played into the regime's hands, the opposition recognized that nonviolent discipline was critical. In reference to the government repression which cost over 300 lives during the

---

21   Interview, Hashim Mattar, Khartoum North, January 8, 2020.

eight-month struggle, businessman and opposition activist Hashim Mattar, whose son was among those killed, noted,

> *Their plan was to compel us to react violently, but from the beginning we understood that the only weapon we have is nonviolence. This is the weapon that we have and they don't. They wanted to put us in a bottle by using violence. We knew that if we reacted with violence we would lose. We understood well that nonviolence is the only 'weapon' that they do not have.*[22]

With a series of horrific civil wars and brutal military dictatorships, the Sudanese had experienced more violence over their 64 years of independence than almost any country in the world, most of it coming from their own government. Yet by 2019, an increasing number of Sudanese recognized that the regime's violence was a sign of its weakness, not its strength. As Yousif noted, "The regime has arms and money, but people have actual power."[23]

Social media was utilized to not only encourage protesters to remain nonviolent but to explain *why* it was important to stay nonviolent. Arabic translations of the writings of Gene Sharp and other scholars documenting the strategic advantages of sustained nonviolent resistance were circulated among protesters, along with online materials provided by international non-governmental organizations discussing the history, theory, and dynamics of strategic nonviolent action.[24] In addition, a few activists attended in-person seminars and workshops on nonviolent organizing in Europe, India, and the United States. Despite this valuable external support, the commitment to nonviolent discipline by the opposition leadership and the ability of millions of Sudanese to heed their calls appears to have been rooted in their own historical experience and strategic calculations.[25]

Enforcing Nonviolent Discipline

A major factor in maintaining nonviolent discipline was the decision by leading activists to make enforcement of nonviolent discipline a high priority among movement participants. Not only was the expectation of nonviolent discipline highlighted in the calls for action, but activists were vigilant in responding to those who acted otherwise. For example, when someone in a crowd would throw an object, engage in other violent activities, or threaten to do so, they would be immediately surrounded by other protesters to prevent them from acting out.

---

22 Ibid.

23 Interview, Khaled Omar Yousif, Khartoum, January 12, 2020.

24 Interviews, ONAD headquarters, Khartoum, January 9, 2020.

25 Ibid.

Given the eight-week, high-risk standoff outside the military headquarters starting in early April 2019, the need for nonviolent discipline on the part of the protesters was especially important. As a result, protesters set up checkpoints around the sit-in area near the military headquarters and elsewhere to frisk would-be protesters to insure they had no weapons or objects that could be used as projectiles, even something as small as a hand mirror.[26] Indeed, if someone wanted to participate in an action which potentially involved direct confrontation with authorities, they would be required to find people who could vouch for them as sincere supporters of the movement. This process served as a means of screening out potential government infiltrators as well as making sure protesters were level-headed and willing to abide by the expectations of not using violence. Sometimes, activists would engage in searches through social media or other means of performing a background check to insure a person's bona fides, sometimes circulating a photo among activists to see if the individual was recognized and make sure they were trustworthy. Such efforts proved to be decisive in maintaining nonviolent discipline in the face of horrific government repression designed to provoke a violent response.

Nonviolent Training

In addition to explicit directives by the FFC, the SPA, and other oppositionists to maintain nonviolent discipline, there were also trainings in nonviolent resistance, particularly during the sit-in in front of military headquarters. Activists were able to share these skills in large part due to work which had been going on for years previously by nominally non-political civil society groups which were not formally part of the FFC. For several years leading up to the revolution, a number of international organizations, such as the U.S. Institute of Peace, led workshops for civil society groups on civic education, conflict resolution, and other issues which likely contributed to the empowerment of activists, though trainings specifically dealing with strategies and tactics of civil resistance were exclusively of Sudanese origin.

One of the groups which played an important role in promoting nonviolent means of resistance was the Organisation for Nonviolence and Development (ONAD; formally known as the Sudanese Organisation for Nonviolence and Development until South Sudan seceded in 2011). Its initial leadership was made up primarily of South Sudanese and has been active in that new country, but its office in Khartoum has continued its work. Since its founding in 1994, ONAD worked with political activists, students and other youth, political parties, and religious leaders, among others. For years, the organization offered workshops throughout the country on such issues as peacebuilding, gender, human rights, civic education, institutional development, good governance, conflict resolution, interfaith dialogue, and group process. Given the destruction of most civil society institutions under the 30-year dictatorship

---

26 Interview, Hashim Mattar, Khartoum North, January 8, 2020.

and the divide-and-rule tactics of the regime, such seemingly apolitical topics ended up having significant political implications. In addition to the trainings in these areas, ONAD also led workshops focusing directly on strategic nonviolent action and maintaining nonviolent discipline in the face of attacks and other provocations by security forces. As the organization continued to publicly emphasize its focus on "nonviolence" to avoid suspicion from authorities, ONAD ended up playing an important role in the resistance committees and direct nonviolent actions of the movement.

While it developed its own curricula, ONAD was influenced by training manuals from various European and Indian groups, including the Gandhian Institute, War Resisters' International, and Swedish Fellowship of Reconciliation. Also valuable were DVDs and other materials documenting civil resistance campaigns and lessons learnt for activists from American educational foundations like the International Center on Nonviolent Conflict and the Albert Einstein Institution. ONAD estimates that it trained at least 10,000 people directly and 50,000 indirectly through its training for trainers. The organization's emphasis on nonviolent action increased over time, with close to 70% of its trainings focused on direct challenges to the government and other oppressive institutions.

As political repression intensified in early 2019 as the movement gained strength, ONAD became targeted for surveillance and a number of its leaders were arrested, forcing them to scale back their direct institutional involvement in the protests. However, individual ONAD staff members remained active with the resistance committees and remained influential despite no longer having a formal role. ONAD also continued to influence the movement through social media, stressing the need for nonviolent discipline.[27]

---

27   Ibid.

Other Factors Contributing to Success

In addition to maintaining nonviolent discipline, there were a number of additional movement-centered factors which contributed to the revolution's success. Structural conditions conducive to resistance were also helpful.

Breadth and Depth of Civil Resistance

A critical factor in the success of the revolution was the scope and scale of the movement. Unlike some civil insurrections—which almost exclusively took place in the capital with mostly middle-class support—the Sudanese revolution took place across the country, in all the different regions, and with diverse class and ethnic participation. Though the Sudanese Professionals Association (SPA) played a key leadership role, local resistance committees (described below) were also active in even the poorest neighborhoods. Indeed, the ability to build such a broad coalition of forces across class lines, the urban/rural divide, and ethnic and regional divisions was vitally important, given the size and complexity of the country.

Unlike some civil insurrections—which almost exclusively took place in the capital with mostly middle-class support—the Sudanese revolution took place across the country, in all the different regions, and with diverse class and ethnic participation.

For decades, the regime had tried to divide Sudanese by North and South, Arab and non-Arab, Muslim and non-Muslim. The pro-democracy protesters recognized that national unity was critically important and consciously resisted the regime's efforts to divide-and-rule. For example, though historically in the predominantly Arab part of the Sudan, greater Khartoum is a multi-ethnic urban area, as those from minority regions fleeing violence and poverty have flocked to the capital over the decades. When the protests began, the regime tried to blame the uprising on the Sudan Liberation Movement, based in Darfur. The Furs, the people indigenous to the Darfur region who had been subjected to a genocidal campaign by the regime, had flocked by the tens of thousands to the Khartoum area over the years to flee the repression. In response, the largely Arab but multi-ethnic protesters began chanting "We are all Darfur!" In solidarity, protesters in Al-Fashir, the Darfur capital, started chanting "We are all Khartoum!" Chants, posters, placards and flags underscored the theme of national unity.[28] As one activist described it,

---

28 For example, the original tri-colored national flag was frequently displayed as a subtle counter to the current flag adopted under the Nimeiry dictatorship (which was designed in a manner similar to Arab states), as a way of recognizing the country's large non-Arab population. Murals sometimes featured the map of the country with its original boundaries including South Sudan, symbolizing that South Sudanese were still welcomed as Sudanese.

*We each have our own favorite slogans from the revolution and mine has always been "*عنصري يا نظام كل البلد دارفور*," loosely translated to "You are a racist regime, we are all Darfur." I traveled to South Sudan and I've been to Darfur many times, and I can tell you that this slogan is something new in Sudan. It's an attempt by youth to try to resolve our big problems historically imposed by past leaders. So, in this revolution these young people have decided they aren't going to be trapped by Bashir's distortion about Arab or African, and instead they resolved the dilemma and said that we are all Sudanese and that is good enough, and the only way to be Sudanese is to understand that the entire country is Darfur.[29]*

Similarly, solidarity across faith traditions and ethnicities was evident during the sit-ins and other sustained actions. In a manner also observed during Egypt's pro-democracy struggle, Christian Sudanese would stand guard securing the boundaries of the areas in which Muslims were praying. Similarly, in poorer neighborhoods, where generations of urban Arabs had recently been joined by displaced persons from Darfur and other rural areas, there was a concerted effort to include everyone in the protests, decision-making, and mutual aid efforts, not just to counter the regime's actions to exacerbate divisions, but to maximize participation, instill collective ownership of the struggle, and create a model of a future democratic Sudan.[30]

Local Resistance Committees

At the heart of the revolution were the local resistance committees. The SPA and other formal opposition groups often lacked representatives on the ground, so the committees worked as their grassroots base, passing on their messages received through social media to neighbors who did not have access to such communication technologies. With the internet blackout following the June 3 massacre, the network of neighborhood committees was critical in coordinating ongoing resistance activities, printing out information and passing it around to local residents and providing VPN addresses to people so they could circumvent the restrictions and get back online. Members of the committees lived in the neighborhoods and villages that they operated in and knew their neighbors, which enabled a degree of trust in the movement that would not have been otherwise possible.

The resistance committees grew out of the 2013 protests and formed loose networks that would engage in periodic small protests, with some tracing their roots as far back as 2008.[31] Much of their activism prior to the revolution was low-key, such as graffiti campaigns.

---

29   Interview, Khalid Medani, Khartoum, January 7, 2020.

30   Interview, popular resistance committee members, Omdurman, January 8, 2020.

31   Claire Debuyser, "'We resist, we build, we watch' – in Sudan, neighbourhood resistance committees are the guardians of the revolution," *Equal Times*, April 9, 2020, **https://www.equaltimes.org/we-resist-we-build-we-watch-in?lang=en#.XriEPHtlDIU.**

The committees were informal, locally autonomous, and covered neighborhoods, villages, and other smaller networks of residents. These were particularly popular among young Sudanese, who did not feel included in the traditional opposition groups or adequately represented in the FFC. These local committees gave the young activists who dominated the revolution a sense of agency, inspiring them to continue the struggle for their own future, a remarkable contrast to the fatalism and sense of powerlessness that had been the hallmark of young Sudanese for decades.

By serving as the main channel of contact between national opposition leaders and the grassroots, leading and organizing local protests, assigning roles and responsibilities, providing a relatively safe space for participation, and monitoring and mitigating state repression, the committees were the key to the revolution's success. The largely poor and working-class leaders of the resistance committees were able to mobilize people in the mostly poor and working-class neighborhoods in ways the middle-class leadership of the SPA would have otherwise found difficult.

Committee members were assigned different tasks, such as serving as medics for the injured, acting as scouts to warn of approaching security forces, being videographers of protests, and preparing masks to protect protesters from tear gas. Having an active role in the movement, as opposed to simply being a passive member of a large crowd, provided participants with a sense of pride and ownership in the struggle which gave the movement and its actions strength beyond its numbers.

This large-scale decentralized network of activists who could organize a protest within minutes helped create a situation where security forces were over-extended and exhausted from having to constantly move from place to place to suppress actions.

By May of 2019, the resistance committees had an elected council at the national level, but were still decentralized and fluid enough to withstand the increased government repression. Waleed Omar, a leader of a resistance committee in Omdurman observed, "There is no single leadership, but instead [the movement relies] on a wide network for coordination. Each area can make their own decisions based on the security situation and other conditions."[32] This decentralization was a major asset, making it difficult for the regime to arrest leaders and cripple the movement. Furthermore, if one neighborhood was experiencing a crackdown from police and other security forces, committees in nearby neighborhoods would immediately mobilize protests to help take the pressure off. This large-scale decentralized network of activists who could organize a protest within minutes helped create a situation where security forces were over-extended

---

32   Interview, Omar Manis, Omdurman, January 11, 2020.

and exhausted from having to constantly move from place to place to suppress actions. Failure to put down a protest would embolden even more people to join in, so the regime found itself in an ongoing dilemma.

The neighborhood resistance committees played a major role in logistics, such as preparing meals for those participating in sit-ins and organizing weekly at-cost food markets to help those dealing with shortages during the disruption of the months-long protests. Not only did such efforts help meet tangible needs, but they gave these committees much greater respectability, particularly in contrast with the notoriously corrupt and inefficient government. The regime had formed what were called "popular committees" in most neighborhoods, but being corrupt and having little credibility, the resistance committees soon supplanted them as the de facto local governing bodies, settling disputes between neighbors and dealing with other everyday matters. They served to organize street cleanup, construction projects, and other local needs, raising funds from fellow residents. They were able to demonstrate that decentralized democratic governance was actually far more efficient than a centralized authoritarian state, serving as a tangible model for a better Sudan.

The Role of Women

Among the Bashir regime's most oppressive policies were those targeting women, who had to endure strict dress codes and limitations on movement without the accompaniment of a close male relative. At the same time, given the traditionally important role of women in Sudanese society, the regime had simultaneously appointed conservative women into political roles to prop up the regime, so having women in active political roles was not a radical departure from the norm. Having women take on such a visible role in the resistance, however, was new.

As many as 70% of the protesters in the streets were reported to be female.[33] Women's participation and leadership not only helped in increasing the numbers of protesters, but provided a perspective that encouraged nonviolent discipline, democratic process, greater credibility, and better popular perception of the movement and its goals. The *zaghareet*, the ululating cry of women common in celebratory occasions in many North African and Middle Eastern societies, was often the signal for the start of protests.

A frequent theme illustrated in murals, signs, and elsewhere during the revolution involved the Kandaka, a matrilineal dynasty of powerful Sudanese queens from the first millennium BC. It served as an inspiration for women and a reminder that the regime's ultra-conservative interpretation of Islam which severely circumscribed their rights was not inherent in Sudanese history or culture.

---

33 "Letter from Africa: 'We're not cleaners' – sexism amid Sudan protests," *BBC News*, April 1, 2019, **https://www.bbc.com/news/world-africa-47738155**.

During the sit-in outside military headquarters, Alaa Salah, a student protester involved with FFC's MANSAM (Women of Sudanese Civic and Political Groups) dressed in the flowing white fabrics associated with the Kandaka, stood on top of a car to give an impromptu speech. The photograph went viral internationally and came to symbolize to many the Sudanese revolution.

Prior to the sit-in, at a time when the uprising appeared to be losing momentum, it experienced a dramatic revival on March 8 in honor of International Women's Day, when women and men marched chanting, "You women, be strong!" and "This revolution is a women's revolution!" The following day, tens of thousands descended upon the main women's prison in Khartoum, leading to the release of all women held in custody for their participation in the protests. While women were underrepresented in the top leadership of the FFC and SPA, overall their role in the Sudanese movement is among the most significant in the history of global pro-democracy struggles.

Effective Messaging

The movement was also successful in challenging the regime's self-justifying propaganda. The military had made an alliance with right-wing Islamists and co-opted Islamist ideology, effectively claiming that since they represented Islamic governance, challenging the regime was therefore anti-Islamic. Pro-democracy activists were able to counter this claim, portraying them not as authentically pious leaders but as "merchants of religion," using Islam as a commodity to solidify their control on power. Among other results, this effort led to some prominent members of the Islamist party's youth wing defecting to the side of the revolution.[34]

Another example of countering the regime's propaganda was exposing false charges against minorities. When Fur students attending university in Khartoum were tortured into making false confessions that they were sent by the Sudan Liberation Movement to incite violent protests, pro-democracy activists responded via a Facebook campaign featuring the students and their friends exposing the regime's lies.[35]

The use of murals to convey solidarity, hope for change, resistance to repression and other inspiring messages sprung up throughout greater Khartoum and in cities and towns across the country. Even for those not actively involved in the struggle, it was a constant reminder that a culture of resistance had emerged in the country and that the relative passivity and acquiescence of recent decades was a thing of the past.

---

34 Interview, Khalid Medani, Khartoum, January 7, 2020.

35 Flora Carmichael and Owen Pinnell, "How fake news from Sudan's regime backfired," *BBC News*, April 25, 2019, https://www.bbc.com/news/blogs-trending-47899076.

Alaa Salah in the image that went viral as a symbol of the Sudanese Revolution

Photo: Lana Haroun (published with permission)

There were also many examples of positive, constructive programming. Each Saturday, under the slogan, "We are going to build it," activists engaged in cleaning up streets and sidewalks, painting walls, and other community projects underscoring that they were connected and committed to the community and that their goal was to build a better society. The collaboration of surrounding neighborhoods to distribute provisions and medical supplies, and to meet the other needs of the many thousands involved in the sit-ins offered a model of an egalitarian democratic system of coordination and distribution, a remarkable shift for those who had known nothing but dictatorship. Indeed, the widespread sense that Sudan's youth were a "lost generation" of lazy, apathetic individuals, disempowered and made narcissistic from living in such a corrupt, inept and repressive political system was shattered. Instead, an image of the empowered youth emerged, risking their lives, assuming leadership, and working hard for a better future for all. They were able to effectively communicate their determination to not miss out on the opportunities lost by their parents' generation.

The respect for youth on the front line became apparent following the killing of the prominent young activist Mohamed Mattar, an engineering student who had returned from graduate school in Britain to join the protest. His murder by government snipers prompted the #BlueforSudan online movement, in honor of his favorite color.[36] Thousands of human rights activists around the world as well as celebrities such as Demi Lovato, Naomi Campbell, and Rhianna changed their social media profiles to blue with the hashtag in honor of Mohamed and in support for the movement, bringing attention to a revolution which until then had received relatively little media coverage in the West.

Social Media

With the regime maintaining strict control on the print and broadcast media, especially as the uprising grew, effective communication within the resistance was critical, particularly given the broad geographical range of the protests. Around the world, social media has become an increasingly important vehicle for ordinary citizens to hold those in power accountable. "It forced the government and the rest of the world to pay attention to us," said Hiba Siddig Diab, a young protester in Khartoum.[37]

Despite the country's poverty, the Sudanese have one of the higher rates of internet connectivity in both Africa and the Arab world at over 30% of the population.[38] With close to one out of every three Sudanese citizens having the capability to keep track of events as they were unfolding, it was relatively easy to spread the word further among friends, neighbors, and family members without internet access.

During the nine-month uprising, a United Nations Development Program study reported that, on Twitter alone, "media files were shared around 400,000 times containing photos, infographics, videos, and images with caricatures and cartoons depicting reality and satires on the ongoing situation."[39] For example, following a protest or major incident with security forces, people would tweet to show solidarity, often including a descriptive hashtag. Similarly, calls for participation in a march, rally, or other action would use a specific hashtag. International news outlets would pick up on the initial posts that would later get circulated and shared further across networks of activists.

The June 3 massacre was live-streamed, helping to turn both Sudanese and international opinion against the TMC. The shutting down of the internet immediately afterwards

---

36   Martin Belem, "#BlueforSudan: social media users show solidarity for protester," *The Guardian*, June 14, 2019, https://www.theguardian.com/world/2019/jun/14/blueforsudan-social-media-users-show-solidarity-for-protester.

37   Alexander Durie, "The Sudan Uprising and the critical role of social media," *The New Arab*, September 17, 2019, https://english.alaraby.co.uk/english/indepth/2019/9/17/sudans-uprising-and-the-critical-role-of-social-media.

38   Telecommunication Development Bureau, "Measuring digital development: Facts and figures 2019," International Telecommunication Union (ITU), 2020, https://www.itu.int/en/ITU-D/Statistics/Pages/facts/default.aspx.

39   United Nations Development Program, Making Sense of Social Media Proxies Findings of Social Media Study on Sudan, 4.

was a setback, yet it also underscored to activists that full access to the internet was not essential to continue the revolution. "We had to go back to very primitive and traditional techniques," said Samahir Elmubarak of the SPA, who noted how it forced them into "going door-to-door, mobilisation through leaflets, through rallies, and this proved very effective because the result was the greatest rally in the history of Sudan on June 30. That was organised without social media."[40]

The important link between the resistance and the Sudanese diaspora community was largely facilitated through social media. The diaspora spread news on social media in other countries, provided financial and other support, and pressured foreign governments to take action. According to Munzoul Assal, director of the Peace Research Institute at the University of Khartoum, "The diaspora played a very significant role in the downfall of Bashir. They were very active in social media, lobbied governments in their new homes, and organised themselves politically by staging demonstrations across Europe, the US and Australia."[41] The Sudanese diaspora also used their social media platforms to engage in fundraising, and other efforts to support the revolution.[42]

There have been some cases of unarmed insurrections where the role of social media has been exaggerated.[43] However, in the case of Sudan, the use of Twitter and other social media platforms really does appear to have played a major role. Still, as the events during the blackout period indicate, it is ultimately people, not technology, that drove the revolution.

Security Force Defections

Except for elite forces like the Rapid Support Forces (RSF), who were largely responsible for the June 3 massacre, demonstrators knew that most security forces were reluctant to support the repression and would refuse orders to shoot or would fire well over the heads of protesters. As a result, while RSF snipers were to be feared, the vast majority of confrontations with police and the regular army did not end with lethal force. One young Sudanese-American who was visiting his grandparents during the uprising and joined in some of the protests

---

40 Alexander Durie, "The Sudan Uprising and the critical role of social media," *The New Arab*, September 17, 2019, **https://english.alaraby.co.uk/english/indepth/2019/9/17/sudans-uprising-and-the-critical-role-of-social-media**.

41 Emma Graham-Harrison, "Sudan's displaced citizens stir revolt from the sidelines," *The Observer*, April 21, 2019, **https://www.theguardian.com/world/2019/apr/21/sudan-diaspora-stir-revolt-from-overseas**.

42 Ismail Kushkush, "Sudan's diaspora has played a crucial role in supporting the anti-Bashir protests," *Quartz Africa*, April 10, 2019, **https://qz.com/africa/1591956/sudans-diaspora-helped-bring-bashirs-end-near/**.

43 See, for example: Laurie Penny, "Revolts don't have to be tweeted: Laurie Penny on a force bigger than technology," *New Statesmen*, February 15, 2011 **https://www.newstatesman.com/blogs/laurie-penny/2011/02/uprisings-media-internet**.

noted, "I actually enjoyed the novelty of running from police and being unafraid of being shot in the back. I can't do that as a young black man in the United States!"[44]

Members of the National Intelligence and Security Service and their RSF fighters were publicly shunned, as were their families, a radical step in a close-knit society. By contrast, members of other security forces without such ideological ties to the regime were encouraged to defect and were offered protection by activists. Defecting soldiers were given sanctuary in homes and, as word got out that protesters were welcoming rather than punishing soldiers who left their units, defections increased. Even soldiers nominally still in their positions engaged in noncooperation. It was not uncommon for an activist to be "arrested" by a soldier, being taken down an alley out of sight of his commanders and then released and told to run away.[45] Security forces would be purposely slow when ordered to deploy or would refuse to move into position altogether. The military received close to 70% of the government's budget, but ordinary soldiers and many junior officers felt exploited and marginalized. With many sharing more in common with the protesters than their superiors, it was not surprising that the regime and the military brass were increasingly concerned about the loyalty of their foot soldiers and recognized that they could not defeat the movement by force.

Tactical Innovations

There have been a number of interesting stories of tactical innovations by protesters, some of which are noted below. An important aspect of the struggle was the decision to engage in actions addressing different issues and mobilizing different constituencies (i.e., women's rights, freeing political prisoners) as well as engaging in a diversity of nonviolent tactics (i.e., marches, rallies, sit-ins, strikes). This approach helped avoid the pitfall experienced by some movements of repeating the same actions over and over, which usually leads to a drop off in participation and momentum.

With neighborhoods under constant guard by security forces, assembling for a demonstration in a normal manner was impossible. To get around that, in the hours before the scheduled start time activists would wander into shops and homes adjacent to the proposed assembly area and hide in backrooms, closets, and storage areas until the appointed time when the sounds of drums, the *zaghareet*, or another signal alerted everyone to pour out at once. While Sudanese society does not generally prioritize punctuality, these protests would routinely begin right on time. This made it very difficult for security forces to prevent protests from starting (particularly since the *zaghareet* could be used to signal many other occasions).

---

44   Interview, Khartoum, January 13, 2020.

45   Interview, Khartoum, January 14, 2020.

Protesters shared various practical tips with each other on how to avoid suspicion if stopped by the omnipresent undercover police, such as hiding cloth masks to protect against teargas in undergarments and avoiding walking with more than one or two other people. One activist noted, "You had to regularly delete photos and videos of protests from your phone, as you would frequently get stopped and thoroughly searched. What came to be known as 'the protest phone' [a secondary phone specifically used for resistance communication] became a necessity."[46]

One important way of convincing authorities that their intimidation was not working was protesters making clear that they were unafraid of being taken to the country's dreaded prisons. When mass arrests at one protest in Khartoum filled all the police vans, ONAD took another van loaded with protesters to the detention center in nearby Omdurman where their arrested comrades were being held. Once the second van arrived at the jail site, they demanded that they be incarcerated as well. As still more prisoners were brought in and as increasingly large crowds of family members and others outside demanded their release, police at the prison ended up releasing previously detained activists since there was not enough room in the jail. At this point, the authorities realized detentions were not working in instilling fear and squashing protests, so they ended up releasing all those arrested during the demonstration. Almost all of the released protesters, including those who had been demonstrating outside, then returned to the original protest site to resume the rally.[47]

The general strike has historically been a critical tactic in bringing down autocratic regimes, including in the 1964 and 1985 uprisings in Sudan. However, the opposition was initially reluctant to utilize this tool, in part because they recognized the relative weakness of the sectoral opposition consisting of unions and other representative professional bodies after thirty years of dictatorship. Without having organized cells within certain sectors of the economy, the opposition recognized that simply making an announcement would not likely trigger a successful strike of the magnitude needed to pressure the regime. An only partially successful general strike would not only be ineffective but could hurt the movement's momentum. They recognized it was easier to organize strikes in specific sectors that the opposition was able to prepare, so they initially engaged in strikes specifically in the industries of engineers, telecommunications workers, non-emergency physicians and others, essentially testing their ability to organize a general strike. Eventually, they had developed the networks and support to launch the two successful general strikes in May and June.

---

46   Reem Abbas, "Sudan's Unfinished Revolution: The Dictator Is Gone, but the Fight Continues," *The Nation*, April 26, 2019.

47   Interview, ONAD headquarters, Khartoum, January 9, 2020.

Structural Factors

Some factors that favored the popular upheaval—though they did not necessarily determine the onset, nature, trajectories, or outcome of the resistance—were structural, either predating the movement's emergence or not being controlled or caused by it.

One advantage in the resisters' favor was that some of the main elements of the repressive apparatus of the regime—the police, intelligence, military, and special forces—were divided, and the opposition did an excellent job of exacerbating those divisions and using them to the movement's advantage. Reem Abbas noted that by the third day of the April sit-in, "it was evident that a significant number of junior army officers were siding with the people. They not only protected them at night from armed assailants, whom people believe were recruited by the NISS, but sent the protesters messages saying they supported them and that they should keep the sit-in going."[48]

> *Businesspeople, even those who had supported the ruling party, realized that—for the sake of the economy and therefore their own self-interest—had to end their support for military rule and support democratic governance.*

An additional factor was that businesspeople, even those who had supported the ruling party, realized that—for the sake of the economy and therefore their own self-interest—they had to end their support for military rule and support democratic governance. Ongoing sanctions, rampant corruption, and internal instability had put the economy into a tailspin and they recognized something had to change. The two general strikes largely shut down the country, underscoring the power of ordinary Sudanese to disrupt the economy. Leaders of the pro-democracy movement met directly with top pro-regime businessmen, including some of the country's leading oligarchs, and were successful in pushing for their change of allegiance.

Another structural factor was the role of international actors. Though Egypt, Saudi Arabia, and the United Arab Emirates backed the TMC with billions of dollars' worth of support, the African Union and European countries were on the movement's side, thanks in part to the efforts of the exile community and others to mobilize their support, making clear that Sudan's pariah status in the international community would not shift without a change in regime.

There was also the fact that the Sudanese regime was simply incompetent. The economy was in shambles. Education, transport, healthcare, agriculture and other basic infrastructure had deteriorated significantly during the regime's three decades in power. This was seen as particularly unfair in light of the fact that the Sudanese had historically made a major

---

[48] Reem Abbas, "Sudan's Unfinished Revolution: The Dictator Is Gone, but the Fight Continues," *The Nation*, April 26, 2019.

contribution to institution building in other Arab countries, sending teachers, engineers and doctors to Libya, Yemen, Saudi Arabia, and other Gulf states. Sudanese universities, once among the most prestigious in the Middle East and Africa, had deteriorated notably due to lack of support and the emigration of leading scholars. They had lost the southern third of the country along with most of the oil reserves when South Sudan became independent in 2011. The regime did not reinvest the remaining oil money. Corruption was rampant. For example, the health minister started his own hospitals, and reallocated scarce resources from state hospitals to support his business venture. Despite its brutality, the regime was in many respects weak.

There seems to have also been a sense, particularly among young Sudanese, that they had simply had enough. Similar to the first Palestinian intifada and the townships uprisings in South Africa during the 1980s, where young people felt they had no future under the status quo and therefore had nothing to lose, Sudanese youth were willing to risk dying rather than continue to live without any hope of a promising future under the current repressive system. For many Sudanese, the struggle was not just political and about injustice in Sudanese society, but profoundly personal.

Post-Revolutionary Transition and the Role of a Mobilized People

The new government which came to power as a result of the revolution has been led primarily by liberal civilian technocrats. The main interim governing bodies consist of the Council of Ministers, the Sovereignty Council, and the Legislative Council in which the military still has strong representation. Elections are scheduled for 2022, by which time pro-democracy activists hope to further civic education and strengthen democratic secular parties in order to successfully counter the military, Islamists, and other anti-democratic forces.

As history has shown in civil resistance struggles around the world, changing a deeply entrenched oligarchy is more difficult than overthrowing a single dictator.

The revolution was, however, not a complete victory. As history has shown in civil resistance struggles around the world, changing a deeply entrenched oligarchy is more difficult than overthrowing a single dictator.

The compromise agreement established executive, quasi-legislative, and constitutional bodies predominately made up of civilians but in which representatives of the military still play a major role. Combined with ministries largely populated by those appointed during Bashir's rule, the interim government has greatly frustrated many Sudanese who hoped to see a large-scale purging of the military from political structures of the state, including elements of the old order from the state bureaucracy.

One problem is that millions of Sudanese, many among the country's best and brightest, went into exile during Bashir's 30-year rule to start new lives. As a result, even though the ministry heads are largely civilians, there is not a large pool of educated people to draw from to fill civil service positions. Consequently, the vast majority of government jobs remain in the hands of those who were appointed during the dictatorship.

Many Sudanese remain traumatized after so many years of repression and are not sure how to act in the context of their new-found freedom. There are efforts by democratic political parties, grassroots activists, and civilians in government to promote civic education and political consciousness raising through workshops and organizing around local issues. Many in the diaspora are returning, at least part time, and contributing financial and other resources to support efforts to rebuild a vibrant civil society. The need to rebuild civil society and not just assume that the only way things can get done is through personal or familial connections with someone in government is an ongoing challenge.

Meanwhile, protests continue, particularly among those seeking justice for civilians killed in the uprising. These protests are in large part not discouraged by government leaders who see such pressure from below as a means of gaining leverage in their battle for influence with holdovers from the old regime still entrenched in government and the security services. One government minister noted that there is still a lot of energy out there, but it needs to be harnessed in a positive direction.[49] However, unlike the 1985-89 period, when the civilian coalition government was weakened by constant strikes, labor activists appear willing to defer badly-needed wage increases and other economic changes in order to give the civilian government a chance in its ongoing struggle with the old guard.

Not all successful pro-democracy civil insurrections are initially clear-cut victories. In countries like Kenya, South Korea, and Brazil, the institutional, constitutional, and legal changes occurred over a protracted period long after the initial civic mobilization. The transition from outright dictatorship to democracy took place over several years, not instantly. Sudan is off to a better start than most of these cases, but the military and Islamists could still make a comeback.

One hopeful sign is that, while the military is still a major player, it is divided. Some members do not want to give back power to civilians, while others—particularly younger officers—recognize that the 30 years of military rule have been a disaster. Under General Bashir's rule, one-third of the country seceded, many young leaders went into exile, the economy tanked, and the country became an international pariah.

Since the overthrow of military rule, there has been a huge change in society in terms of social freedom. More than just being able to talk politics without fear of the consequences, the omnipresent fear that governed virtually every social interaction is gone. There is no longer the constant sighting of security forces or the fear of undercover police. The Sudanese, particularly women, are acting far friendlier and more outgoing. Until the COVID pandemic hit, social gatherings and meet ups at restaurants and on the street became far more common. A number of Sudanese noted how one could even see the difference in people's posture since they were no longer afraid or on guard. Said one Sudanese-Canadian on a return visit, "You see people are smiling more than in 30 years. Prior to the revolution, unless it's your family, people weren't trusting each other at all. If you needed a taxi, you didn't know who the driver worked for. But now you can say what you want. I have never been happier."[50]

In 1964 and in 1985, the Sudanese people rose up to oust military dictatorships and establish civilian rule only to have their democratic governments overthrown in military coups less than five years later. This is very much on the minds of the Sudanese, along with a strong sense of uneasiness about how long this democratic experiment will last. As a result, many

---

49   Interview, Office of the Prime Minister, Khartoum, January 7, 2020.

50   Interview, Khalid Medani, Khartoum, January 7, 2020.

Map of the Republic of Sudan

Credit: UN Office for the Coordination of Humanitarian Affairs (OCHA)
License: CC BY 3.0, https://creativecommons.org/licenses/by/3.0

are trying to apply the lessons from these past reversals in the hopes of developing means to counter regression, such as avoiding divisive political battles among pro-democracy groups and refraining from labor strikes and other disruptive activities that could weaken the civilian-led government, as well as exploring contingency plans for massive resistance in the face of a coup attempt.

Despite these concerns, many Sudanese expressed optimism about why this time should be different and a democratic transition more permanent. One reason is that the previous uprisings were led by opposition political parties and well-established sectoral groups. The recent revolution, however, was led by youth, it was more organic and grassroots-driven and forced the established opposition parties to be bolder in their demands, less prone to compromise, and more creative in their tactics. The SPA, opposition parties, and other older established oppositionists knew that they could not make a deal that was unacceptable to the neighborhood resistance committees and youth activists who made it possible for them to be at the negotiating table. As one veteran official put it, rather than the previous movements led by prominent opposition politicians and union leaders, "This time, it was more personal, in people's own hands. There was individual ownership of the revolution."[51] Another difference is that the protests in 1964 and 1985 were centered almost exclusively in Khartoum and neighboring Omdurman, while this time they were throughout the country, including smaller cities and rural areas. In addition, while the previous revolutions lasted less than two weeks, the 2018-19 revolution took more than eight months, giving time for civic education, consciousness-raising, and related political activities continue. It is perhaps significant that the 1985 uprising which toppled Jaafar Nimeiry, the Sudanese autocratic president in power since 1969, was referred to as the "intifada" (literally meaning "shaking off") whereas this uprising is referred to as the "revolution." Resistance committees are still active in neighborhoods and independent labor unions, now legal, are coming back to life. There is a real hope that civil society will be strong enough to act as a deterrent against the military taking back rule over the country. They are making it clear to the military that if it tries to seize power, they are not going to quietly go home.

---

51   Interview, Omar Manis, Omdurman, January 11, 2020.

Lessons Learned

There are a number of important lessons to be drawn from the success of the Sudanese revolution, not only for students of civil resistance movements, but for pro-democracy activists confronting autocratic regimes elsewhere in the world.

Commitment to Strategic Nonviolent Conflict

Security force defections, the breadth and depth of the movement, the role of women, and tactical innovations all played a critical role, as did support from the international community, the Sudanese diaspora, and key business leaders. These factors would likely not have come into play were it not for the strict commitment to nonviolent strategies and tactics insisted upon by the movement leadership, and the inclusion of nonviolent training and the enforcement of nonviolent discipline. It is ironic that movements in countries with far more resources, less repression, greater homogeneity, and other supposed advantages often succumb to the call by some activists for "diversity of tactics" or "justified defense," ranging from vandalism and attacks against security personnel to armed struggle—unwilling to enforce nonviolent discipline within their ranks.

The flexibility and willingness to shift and diversify nonviolent tactics as needed, prevented the movement from stagnating and kept the regime struggling to find new ways to respond.

Poverty and Poor Infrastructure Not an Obstacle

Sudan's successful revolution has also challenged the myth that civil resistance cannot work in impoverished countries with high illiteracy rates and poor infrastructure. Sudan is one of the poorest countries in the world, exacerbated by rampant corruption, drought, and—despite being one of the largest countries in Africa—a lack of adequate transport and other basic infrastructure. Its literacy rate is among the lowest in the Arab world. The country ranks near the bottom of the Human Development Index. Despite this, millions of people successfully mobilized across the country.

The Importance of Skills and Agency

In the debate among social movement theorists regarding the relative importance of structural factors versus agency and conditions versus skills, the case of Sudan seems to underscore the importance of skills and agency. As noted above, Sudan was often seen as a hopeless case in terms of democratic change due to the powerful coalition of conservative Islamists and military officers, the weakness of the opposition, and the degree of oppression, ethnic division, poverty, and poor infrastructure, thereby failing the standard criteria for democratic change by traditional theorists of democracy. However, millions of ordinary Sudanese civilians were nevertheless able to organize, mobilize, and follow through to oust the old regime and bring to power a civilian-led government.

Decentralization

Decentralizing the protests insured high levels of participation by enabling people to not have to travel great distances. By spreading the actions out too widely to be easily suppressed, they became relatively low-risk, thereby encouraging even greater numbers. Participation can provide a sense of ownership of a movement and data has shown that numbers can be a critical variable in the success of an insurrection. The flexibility and willingness to shift and diversify nonviolent tactics as needed, prevented the movement from stagnating and kept the regime struggling to find new ways to respond.

Balance of Organizational Leadership and Grassroots Activism

Part of the credit goes to the movement having both the strong leadership of the Sudanese Professionals Association and other established opposition groups which could coordinate the resistance on a national level and the resistance committees in neighborhoods and villages at the grassroots level. The Sudanese appear to have found the right balance between effective organizational leadership providing overall direction and strategy and the more spontaneous direct action oriented by youth, such as in the resistance committees.[52]

Persistence in the Face of Severe Repression

It has long been assumed, despite scores of autocratic governments being ousted through civil resistance movements, that nonviolent strategies and tactics simply cannot work against highly-repressive regimes. Sudan, however, has long been ranked among the half dozen most violent, totalitarian regimes in the world.[53] Bashir has been indicted by the International Criminal Court on multiple counts of genocide, crimes against humanity, and other war crimes, and other top military leaders have been implicated as well. Pro-democracy activists were gunned down in the streets of Khartoum and other cities, yet the protests continued.

Addressing the movement's tenacity in the face of repression, one of the Forces of Freedom and Change leaders described the importance of continuing to organize even after the June 3 massacre:

---

[52] See Mark Engler and Paul Engler, *This is an Uprising: How Nonviolent Revolt Is Shaping the Twenty-First Century* (Nation Books, 2016).

[53] Michael J. Abramowitz, "Freedom in the World 2018: Democracy in Crisis," *Freedom House*, **https://freedomhouse.org/report/freedom-world/2018/democracy-crisis.**

People after June 3rd [the day of the massacre] felt they were defeated. The psychological effect of 30th of June [the day of the largest protest] was that we returned the power back to our hands. Everyone in the country felt that we either live or we die, but this is the day we have to return back to streets and prove that we are powerful, united and we are going all the way. The military came to the conclusion that they could not continue to rule the country and signed the agreement a week later.[54]

Responding to Disproportionate Violence by Escalating Nonviolent Resistance

There have been some noted cases of mass killings of nonviolent protesters, such as China's 1989 Tiananmen Square massacre, in which the movement gave up, or South Africa's 1960 Sharpeville massacre, in which the movement shifted to an armed struggle. By contrast, the escalation in violent repression by the Sudanese regime led to an escalation of the nonviolent resistance. By succeeding in a struggle against a literally genocidal regime, the Sudanese have demonstrated that few pro-democracy activists can use the excuse that their government is too repressive to contemplate nonviolent resistance. The Sudanese recognized that the most powerful weapons against extreme violence are organized and strategically directed nonviolent mobilization and actions.

---

54   Interview, Khaled Omar Yousif, Khartoum, January 12, 2020.

Conclusion

The serious problems still plaguing Sudan despite a return to civilian leadership should not be underestimated. However, the nonviolent revolution which toppled the Bashir regime and ended direct military rule is one of the most important political events of recent decades. Due to its broader implications, the revolution in Sudan deserves further serious study and analysis. Given its size and significance, the Sudanese revolution did not receive as much media coverage in the United States and other Western countries as it deserved, perhaps because the idea of an Arab people, a Muslim people, and an African people having agency, thinking strategically, and effectively utilizing nonviolent action simply does not fit into the Western narrative.[55]

That should not stop scholars and activists from learning from the Sudanese, however. Given the enormous obstacles to a successful revolution that the people of Sudan were nevertheless able to overcome, the pro-democracy struggle in Sudan should serve as an inspiration for the entire world. If it could happen there, it could happen almost anywhere.

---

55 Mitchell Plitnick, "The Sudanese Ousted a Dictator Last Year—Why Is Washington Still Imposing Sanctions?" *The Nation*, March 20, 2020.

About the Author

Stephen Zunes is a Professor of Politics and International Studies at the University of San Francisco, where he served as founding director of the program in Middle Eastern Studies. Professor Zunes serves as a senior policy analyst for the Foreign Policy in Focus project of the Institute for Policy Studies, an associate editor of *Peace Review*, and a contributing editor of *Tikkun*. He is the author of hundreds of articles for scholarly and general readership on Middle Eastern politics, civil resistance, U.S. foreign policy, and human rights. He is the principal editor of *Nonviolent Social Movements* (Blackwell Publishers, 1999), the author of *Tinderbox: U.S. Middle East Policy and the Roots of Terrorism* (Common Courage Press, 2003), the author of *Civil Resistance Against Coups: A Comparative and Historical Perspective* (ICNC Press, 2017), and co-author (with Jacob Mundy) of *Western Sahara: War, Nationalism and Conflict Irresolution* (Syracuse University Press, second edition, 2021).

www.ingramcontent.com/pod-product-compliance
Lightning Source LLC
Chambersburg PA
CBHW042016120526
44592CB00043B/2963